# CRIMEBUSTERS

## How science fights crime

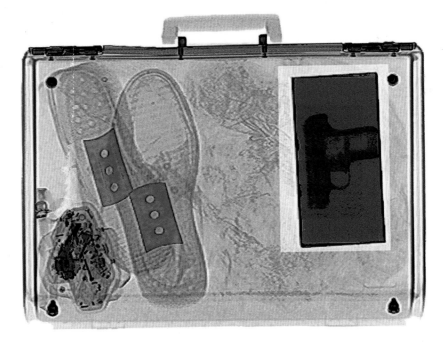

# CRIMEBUSTERS

## How science fights crime

OXFORD

UNIVERSITY PRESS

# OXFORD
## UNIVERSITY PRESS

Great Clarendon Street, Oxford OX2 6DP

Oxford University Press is a department of the University of Oxford.
It furthers the University's objective of excellence in research,
scholarship, and education by publishing worldwide in

Oxford   New York

Auckland   Cape Town   Dar es Salaam   Hong Kong   Karachi
Kuala Lumpur   Madrid   Melbourne   Mexico City   Nairobi
New Delhi   Shanghai   Taipei   Toronto

With offices in

Argentina   Austria   Brazil   Chile   Czech Republic   France   Greece
Guatemala   Hungary   Italy   Japan   Poland   Portugal   Singapore
South Korea   Switzerland   Thailand   Turkey   Ukraine   Vietnam

Oxford is a registered trade mark of Oxford University Press
in the UK and in certain other countries

Text © Oxford University Press 2007

The moral rights of the author have been asserted

Database right Oxford University Press (maker)

First published 2006

British Library Cataloguing in Publication Data

Data available

ISBN 978-0-19-911495-5

10 9 8 7 6 5 4 3 2 1

Originated by Oxford University Press
Created by Harris & Wilson

Printed in Thailand by Imago

Paper used in the production of this book is a natural,
recyclable product made from wood grown in sustainable forests.
The manufacturing process conforms to the environmental
regulations of the country of origin.

# Contents

# Caught!

Thousands of crimes are committed every day. To solve many of these cases, investigators turn to forensic science – the application of science and scientific techniques during a criminal investigation. From identifying a murder victim to the detection of illegal drugs, forensic science plays a central role in crime-fighting.

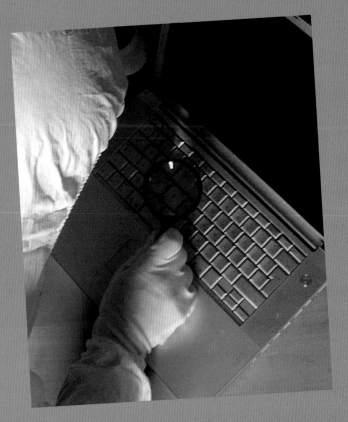

## Crime life-cycle
In television dramas that features forensic science, most cases are solved very quickly. In reality, many cases can take months, and sometimes years, of painstaking work before a person is charged.

## Crime committed
Some crimes occur on the spur of the moment. For example, an argument can turn into a violent assault. Others, however, such as an armed robbery may be planned well in advance. The criminal may be acting alone, or have the help of other people, called accomplices.

## Crime discovered, police alerted
Once alerted, police attend the crime scene. The first law-enforcers to reach the scene secure it and make sure that potential evidence is not disturbed.

## Crime scene investigation
Investigators begin their work at the crime scene which is dusted for fingerprints and photographed. Evidence such as a weapon, clothing or blood is taken back to forensic laboratories for analysis.

## Witnesses and suspects
Officers also seek out witnesses to the crime. They try to narrow down the number of people they believe may have committed the crime, known as suspects.

## Gathering evidence

Suspects may be questioned and their backgrounds checked. Police often obtain permission to check bank balances, telephone records and search properties to seek out further proof.

## Arrested and charged

When investigators believe they have enough evidence, they locate, arrest and charge a suspect. This person is likely to appear in court as the defendant.

## In court

The people in court representing the authorities are called the prosecution. They need to prove the defendant committed the crime by presenting the evidence that has been collected for the case.

## Verdict and sentence

The court makes its verdict – the decision whether the defendant is guilty or innocent. If the defendant is found guilty, sentencing follows. This can range from a warning, known as a caution, to a period in prison.

# What is evidence?

From an abandoned getaway car to a human hair, evidence comes in many different shapes, sizes and forms. Evidence is used by detectives in a number of ways. These include establishing identities of those at the crime scene, linking a suspect to the victim, crime or crime scene, and proof that a witness's statement is accurate. Evidence can also help rule someone out of an investigation.

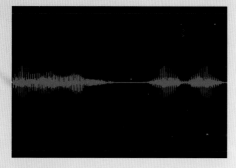

▲ A voice spectrograph produces a voiceprint. People's voices are distinctive but voice analysis is only allowed as evidence in some courts.

## Types of evidence

Not all evidence consists of physical objects such as clothing, bullets or shards of glass. Fingerprint and footprint evidence, crime scene photos and digital evidence taken from computer hard drives can all be crucial. Important evidence often comes from the testimonies of people who either witnessed the crime being committed or tell police about the activities of a particular person.

## Building a case

It's rare for a single piece of evidence to result in a crime being solved. Usually, detectives have to build up a big picture of events before, during and after the crime was committed. Every piece of evidence has to be carefully recorded and stored so that it is admissable in a court of law.

▶ A forensics officer collects evidence from a broken window. The glass fragments might be matched to ones later found on a suspect's clothing. There may also be traces of the object which hit the glass.

▲ A police diver emerges from a river after conducting an underwater search for clues. Any potential evidence found will be taken to the crime lab for further investigation.

## Trace evidence

Trace evidence is an important part of every investigation. Locard's Principle, named after Dr Edmond Locard (1877–1966), a French forensics expert, states that every contact leaves a trace. This means that a criminal will both bring something into the scene (such as a footprint), and leave with something from the scene (such as mud, or a victim's hair or blood).

▲ Careful forensic examination of a computer might lead to the discovery of evidence in the form of a fingerprint, hair or fibre from the clothes of a suspect.

## On the case

A coin was vital evidence that led to the capture of a major spy. In 1953, a newspaper delivery boy in New York received an odd coin as change. The nickel was hollow and contained a microphotograph in code. Four years of investigations eventually led to the unmasking of Rudolf Abel, a Soviet Union spy working in the United States.

# The crime scene

▲ The ruler provides a scale to measure a bloody shoeprint. This may later be matched with a suspect's shoe.

A murder victim has been discovered and pronounced dead. The first priority is to seal off and secure the scene to protect the evidence. Next, investigators photograph the scene exactly as they found it. Then they identify and label any evidence – a single hair or blood stain may be enough to connect a suspect with the murder.

▲ Every piece of evidence is bagged, sealed and labelled. Strict guidelines are followed as this evidence may be used in court.

## Photography

Hundreds of photographs are taken at the crime scene, many of which may later be used in court as evidence. Entry and exit routes are photographed as well as all items found near the scene. Sometimes, video cameras are also used to capture a scene.

## Under the weather

Time is a particular pressure when the crime scene is outdoors. If it rains, for example, vital evidence such as blood may be washed away. The detective in charge has to make decisions about what evidence to protect and preserve first.

## Storing evidence

Officers use gloves when they need to handle evidence but prefer to collect items with tweezers or similar tools. Objects are usually placed in specially sealed bags and tubes that are labelled. Laboratory examination of the evidence may make it possible to link an item with a suspect.

▲ Items found next to the body are carefully numbered. The information stored on a computer database for use during the investigation.

► Protective clothing ensures that any evidence does not become contaminated by dust and hair from the officer's own clothes.

# Investigate

Turn your bedroom into a crime scene. You will need clear plastic bags, paper, a tape measure, masking tape, tweezers and kitchen tongs.

**1** Tape off the entry and exit points using masking tape.

**2** Make a detailed sketch of the scene and note down important 'evidence' (for example, clothing on the floor) and the room's measurements.

**3** Collect a few pieces of evidence, without touching them, using the tweezers or kitchen tongs. Each should be placed into its own clear plastic bag which can be labelled for later investigation.

# Back at the lab

After a crime scene has been carefully examined, most of the physical evidence that has been collected is sent to forensics laboratories. Here, scientists and criminologists get to work. This includes identifying substances, such as blood or poison, analysing objects and recovering evidence, such as hair and fibres from clothes, and matching evidence from the crime scene to a particular person.

▲ Samples of blood, collected from a crime scene, are prepared at a crime laboratory for analysis. Tests can establish if the blood comes from a human and to which blood group it belongs.

## Chain of custody

Evidence is stored and labelled to help provide what is called the chain of custody. The names of everyone who handles a piece of evidence are documented at every stage. If the chain of custody is unclear, or worse, it is shown that evidence has been tampered with, a court may throw the the case out.

## Departments

Most large crime labs have a number of departments specialising in different fields. These usually include firearms matching, fingerprinting and chemical analysis of poisons (known as toxicology). Forensic laboratories also collaborate with other police forces and other labs around the country.

▲ In 1988 Pan Am Flight 103 exploded in mid-air over Lockerbie, Scotland, killing the crew, 259 passengers and 11 people on the ground. Almost 13,000 pieces of evidence from the wreckage were analysed. In 2001, a Libyan terrorist was convicted of planting a bomb on the plane.

## Following leads
When a piece of evidence is believed to be crucial, crime labs go to great lengths to trace its origin and owner. Detailed forensic analysis of a printed letter, for example, may help investigators identify the paper, ink or toner manufactuer and the exact machine it was printed on.

▶ A forensic scientist at a crime lab uses an ultraviolet (UV) lamp to search for biological stains such as blood, sweat or fingerprints.

## The long game
Patience and perseverance are the hallmarks of dedicated forensic scientists. Tests and analysis of evidence can take a long time and there may be many blind alleys before a breakthrough is made. Some cases remain open for many years and are revisited when new techniques such as DNA testing (*see* pp54–55) are developed.

## On the case
The son of the famous aviator, Charles Lindbergh, was kidnapped in 1932 and later found dead. Analysis of the homemade ladder used by the kidnapper to gain entry to the house traced the wood to a particular lumber mill but then the trail went cold. Later, a suspect, Bruno Hauptman (right) was found with some of the paid ransom money. Analysis showed that a missing wooden floorboard in his house had been used to make part of the ladder and that a plane tool in his garage had been used to smooth the ladder. Hauptman was convicted of the crime in 1936.

# What they say

When a serious crime such as a murder or armed robbery occurs, police appeal for witnesses to come forward. Some of the statements given by witnesses help investigators narrow down their search for the criminal. Some witnesses may be asked to appear in court to give testimony. Witness statements may also be used in court alongside forensic evidence.

▼ A witness to a crime is interviewed by a police officer. Even for a single crime, hundreds of statements may be taken.

## Witness evidence

Investigators question witnesses to describe what they heard and saw in as much detail as possible. At a later date, witnesses may be asked to identify a suspect from a police line-up, which consists of innocent people as well as one or more suspects.

## Background checks

Checks are made to see if suspects or victims have previous criminal records. Detectives also visit workplaces, friends and families to build up a detailed picture of the individuals involved. As well as looking for crucial evidence, detectives try to establish a prime reason, or motive, for the crime.

▲ A crime victim and police artist work together to create an identikit face of a criminal. The computer-based system can mix and match facial shapes and features to produce an accurate likeness.

## Questioning suspects

When a suspect is taken into a police station for questioning, officers follow a strict set of interview rules, which differ from country to country. In the UK, for example, an accurate record must be made of every interview, when it starts and ends, and who was present.

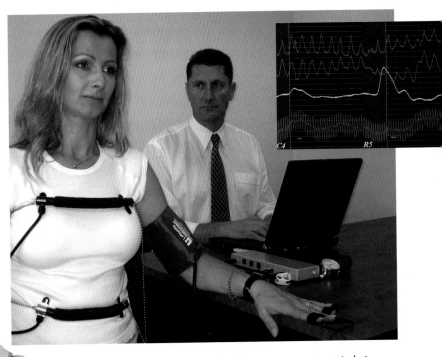

▲ A polygraph, or lie detector, measures vital signs (*above right*) such as hearbeat, skin temperature and blood pressure. When a question is asked and answered, changes in these meaurements may indicate the person is lying.

## On the case

For almost two decades, a mystery bomber, known as the Unabomber, sent explosive devices to university and airport staff killing 3 people and injuring almost 30 others. In 1995, he stated that he would only end his bombing campaign if a major newspaper published some of his writings. When his demands were met, David Kaczynski recognised the writing style of his elder brother, Ted, and told the authorities. Ted Kaczynski was eventually arrested, found guilty of the bombings and was sentenced to life imprisonment.

# Why identify?

Establishing the identities of people involved in a crime is essential to crime-solving success. Physical descriptions are often crucial but other clues, such as fingerprints, can be just as useful. Sometimes, it's not only suspects who need to be tracked down. Corpses cannot always be identified immediately – for example, a fire can burn a body beyond recognition. However, even in these cases, forensic scientists have a range of techniques at their disposal to establish a victim's identity.

◄▲ Closed Circuit Television (CCTV) cameras are found in great numbers in many towns and cities. There are over 3 million CCTV cameras in the UK. They are used for both crime prevention and detection, such as recording this car break-in (above).

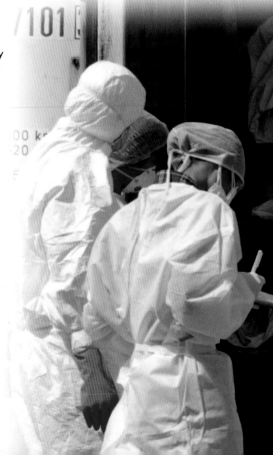

▼ Forensic examination can establish the identities of people killed in natural disasters as well as victims of crime. Here, doctors in Thailand are involved in the painstaking process of identifying some of the many thousands of people killed by the Asian Tsunami of December 2004.

## Clues to identity

Forensic scientists are called in when there is a body or human remains to examine. Vital information about victims and suspects can also be gathered from sources such as clothing, fingerprints, an abandoned car, luggage or weapon. Mobile phone photographs or footage from CCTV cameras often prove invaluable. After bombs were detonated in London in July 2005, police analysed 2,500 hours of CCTV footage to identify the four suspect bombers.

▶ Armed with a police artist's sketch, officers conduct door-to-door enquiries close to the scene of the crime. The sketch may prompt people into recalling when and where they sighted the individual.

## Seeking out witnesses

If a serious crime has been committed, police sometimes make public appeals for witnesses to come forward. They may also conduct house-to-house enquiries. Often, people may not have seen the crime but may have watched crucial events unfold before or after a crime. Witnesses are prompted to give as much information as possible.

## Marked out

Witness descriptions or distinguishing marks, such as unusual scars or tattoos, can lead investigators straight to a suspect. In December 2005 eight members of a drug-trafficking gang were identified by their bat tattoos. Other distinctive features may lie beneath the skin. For example, bodies can be identified by cosmetic implants or metal joint pins used to mend fractures in bones. These show up in X-rays and can be traced to the hospital or clinic where they were originally fitted.

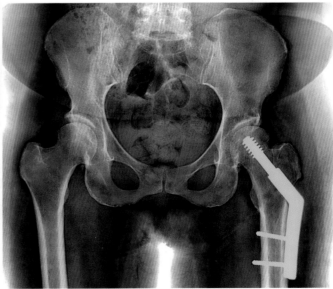

▲ Implants, such as this surgical hip screw revealed by an X-ray, can be traced back to medical records. These can provide crucial information about a victim's identity.

# Fingerprints

Each of your fingertips has a unique pattern of fine ridges that is different to anyone else's – not even identical twins possess the same prints. Analysing these ridges and patterns gives law enforcers a powerful tool for identifying an individual from fingerprints found at a crime scene or elsewhere.

### Fingerprint pioneer

In 1901, the first Fingerprint Bureau was opened in London. Sir Edward Henry, who had developed a system of classifying prints, was put in charge of three special fingerprinting officers. The following year, house burglar Harry Jackson became the first person in the UK to be convicted with fingerprint evidence. Henry's 'ten-print' method of classifying prints was quickly adopted in the USA and many other countries.

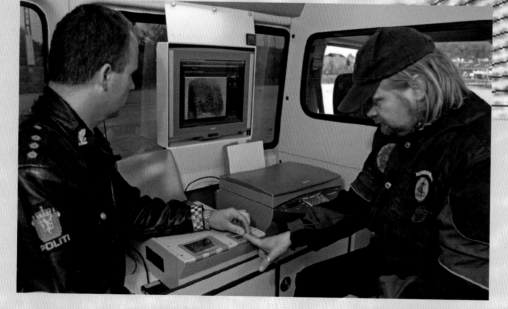

▲ Analysis of a fingerprint scan seeks out unique features of ridges such as where they end (marked in green) and where two lines join (marked in yellow), which is known as bifurcation. A number of these features must be found in the same position to produce a positive identification.

▲ When a suspect (right) is arrested, their prints are taken. In the past fingers were inked and prints placed on cards. Today, many law enforcement forces scan the suspect's fingerprints electronically so that they can be processed immediately.

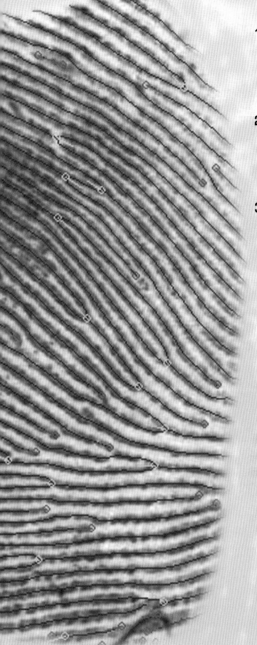

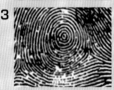

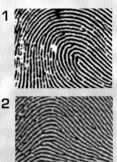

▲ Fingerprints are characterised by the patterns made by ridges. These can include loops (1), arches (2) and whorls (3). Loops are the most common pattern but they vary greatly in size and shape.

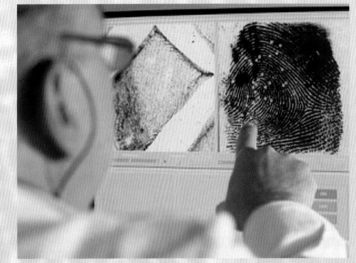

▲ A forensic scientist points out key ridge features of a fingerprint being matched with one held on a database.

## Computer power

Automated fingerprint identification systems (AFIS) speed up the process of comparing and matching prints using powerful computer databases to search and compare. The world's largest database is the FBI's Integrated AFIS (IAFIS). It holds fingerprint records of over 47 million people. An average 6,000 new records are added each day whilst as many as 3,000 searches can be performed every second.

## Record and compare

Prints at a crime scene are matched with ones held on file by seeking out matches of ridge features in the same position on the print. Different countries require different numbers of matches for the evidence to be admissible in court. France and Australia, for example, require 12 points to match but Italy requires 16 points.

## On the case

Painkillers laced with the deadly poison, cyanide, killed two Americans in 1986. Police were closing in on their number one suspect, Stella Nickell, but needed more evidence. From her public library records, they discovered she had taken out books on poisoning – *Human Poisoning* and *Deadly Harvest*. The FBI discovered 84 of her fingerprints mainly on pages about cyanide poisoning. In 1988, she was found guilty and sentenced to 90 years in prison.

# Recovering prints

The forensics team have entered the crime scene. One of their first jobs is to search for fingerprints. Surfaces and objects which investigators think are linked with the crime come under the most intense scrutiny. Some fingerprints are easy to spot and leave a clear mark, such as when hands have had paint, mud or blood on them. Others, which might be invisible to the naked eye, are called latent prints. These can be made visible, however, with dusting powders, chemicals and special lighting.

▲ A computer keyboard is dusted for prints. Detectives use different types of powders – white, black and coloured – to make the prints stand out clearly.

## Powder

One of the most common techniques used to recover fingerprints is dusting. A fine powder is sprinkled or brushed onto an area. Fingerprints contain oils, sweat and other moist substances to which the powder sticks. When the excess dust is brushed away, the print is revealed.

▲ A special fluorescent light source causes fingerprints that are invisible in normal light to glow. Sometimes, dusting powders that contain fluorescent chemicals are used.

## Lifting prints

Some surfaces, such as many types of paper, are porous. This means they absorb moisture which makes it difficult to make prints. However, special magnetic powders can be used on these surfaces to recover fingerprints. Once prints have been powdered, forensic officers at a crime scene often use low-tack sticky tape to 'lift' the print. This can be attached to a clear plastic sheet for safekeeping as important evidence.

## Superglue

Some prints aren't easy to see even after dusting. But superglue can detect extremely faint prints! Surfaces to be checked for prints are placed in a special container together with drops of liquid superglue. The glue is then heated until it becomes a gas. The chemicals in the glue react with traces of chemicals in fingerprints and moisture in the air. This reaction produces a sticky white material that forms along the ridges and reveals the fingerprint.

◄ A forensic officer dusts a handprint with white aluminium powder. The powder sticks to the grease and sweat from the hand, revealing a unique ridged pattern.

## Investigate

You will need:
A very soft paintbrush, a clean glass, some clear sticky tape, a piece of card, and some hot chocolate (cocoa) powder.

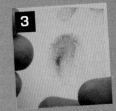

**1** Touch the sides of the glass with your fingers, then sprinkle cocoa powder over the surface.

**2** Brush the cocoa powder away with your soft brush.

**3** Carefully place a piece of tape (sticky side down) on the dusted fingerprint. Lift off the tape and place it on the piece of card to preserve the print.

# Down in the mouth

Many criminals have given themselves away with their mouths, or, more precisely, their lips and teeth. Lip prints taken from a glass, for example, can establish if someone was present at a crime scene. During a stuggle a victim might be left with a bite mark that can be matched to a suspect. As well as identifying the living, teeth can also help identify the dead.

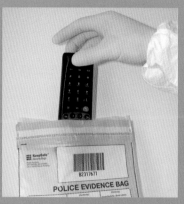

◀ A telephone, with a built-in answering machine, is bagged and taken away as evidence. Messages may contain important information and voices may be identified.

▲ A bite mark (indicated on the transparent overlay) has been used to create this plaster impression.

◀ When you take a bite from an apple, your teeth leave a distinctive pattern.

## Teeth and lips

Teeth marks can be almost as revealing as fingerprints. The size and shape of teeth, their arrangement, the number of fillings or other dental work, help to make each set unique. Lip shape and the patterns on the surface of the lips also vary greatly between people.

## Incriminating bite

Forensic dentistry has had notable successes in matching bite marks to particular people. For example, in 1967, the murderer of Linda Peacock left a bite mark that indicated the biter suffered from a rare disorder that causes pitted teeth. Other evidence led detectives to a young offender's institution in Scotland. The teeth of one of the inmates, Gordon Hay, matched the bite marks and he was convicted of the murder.

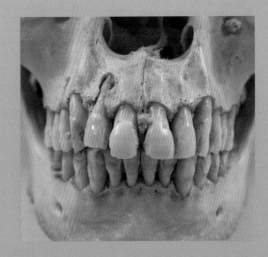

▼ When a murder victim has not been identified, an X-ray of the teeth can provide crucial clues. Forensic dentists compare the teeth and the way they are arranged with dental records to seek out a match.

▶ Teeth are extremely tough parts of the body that remain intact long after a person's death. They can even survive fierce fires that are hot enough to turn bones into ash.

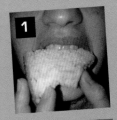

## Estimating age

When a body is discovered, forensic dentists are often called in. They take X-rays, measurements and may make models of the complete upper and lower sets of teeth. The age of a child or adult can be estimated from the growth of teeth, their condition, and whether wisdom teeth are present or have been extracted.

## Investigate

You will need two or more friends, an apple or slice of bread, foam plates or trays, a magnifying glass.

**1** Ask one of your friends secretly to take a bite from the apple or bread.

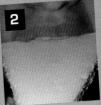

**2** Cut out two wedge-shaped pieces of foam tray and place them together. Ask the suspects to place the tray pieces in their mouth and to bite gently down on each piece. Label each set with the person's name and upper or lower set.

**3** Using a magnifying glass compare the bite marks of your suspects with the bite marks on the food. See if you can get a match.

# Silent identity

A body has been recovered from a crime scene. One of the most important tasks for forensic scientists is to investigate how the person died. Experts, called forensic pathologists, seek out the cause of death, and other clues that will tell them more about the victim.

## Giving up secrets

An autopsy, or post-mortem, is the detailed examination of a body after death. During an autopsy, tell-tale marks, such as gunshot wounds or bruises, might be found that point to the cause of death. Internal organs are also examined for clues that show how a person died.

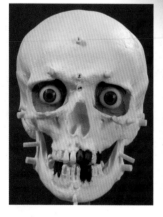

▲ 3-D facial reconstruction starts with an accurate plaster cast of the skull being made. Pegs called tissue markers show the depth of muscles and flesh.

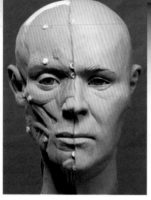

▲ The muscles of the face are moulded from clay and added (left side) to build up the face. A smooth finish is used to mimic skin (right side).

▲ Details such as hairstyle are added to complete the reconstruction. Photographs are circulated in the media and, in some cases, the person may be recognized.

## Making faces

Creating a likeness of a person from a skull is called facial reconstruction. Heads are modelled in clay, as well as recreated on computer. Reconstructions can result in people coming forward to provide the identity of a missing person.

## Time of death

Pathologists take into account a number of factors to establish time of death. These include loss of heat from the body, the condition of partly-digested foods and whether stiffness (*rigor mortis*) has set into the body. Determining the time of death can be crucial in some murder investigations. Suspects, for example, may have alibis that confirm they could not have been present when the victim died.

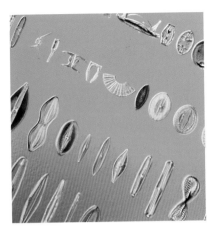

◄ Diatoms are single-celled algae found in rivers, lakes and oceans. Diatoms in the body of a drowned person can sometimes be traced back to a particular place to confirm where the person died.

**4**

**5**

▲ Marks made on the body are examined during an autopsy to establish how the victim died. Injuries might include severe bruising (1), and wounds caused by a shotgun (2), a knife (3 and 5) and a gunshot (4).

## On the case

Forensic science was used to solve the mystery of of a well-preserved body discovered in a Danish bog in 1950. The figure, known as Tollund Man, was found to be over 2,200 years old. Marks on the skin under the chin and sides of the neck showed that the likely cause of death was hanging. Internal investigation indicated the contents of his last meal: seeds including barley and linseed, and a soup made from vegetables.

## Old bones

The use of fingerprints and advances in DNA profiling (*see* pages 54–55) have enabled many unknown bodies to be identified. However, other techniques are still used, especially when the victim died long ago. Even if only a partial skeleton remains, forensic anthropologists can analyse bones to determine the victim's age, gender, height, health and even the cause of death.

# The heat is on

Heat can provide valuable clues for forensic scientists and detectives – from estimating the time of death to detecting a hidden fugitive at night. Detectives arriving at a crime scene also look out for tell-tale instances of heat. Heat from an oven or warm food or drinks, for example, are signs that someone was present only moments earlier.

▼ In a thermal image, or thermogram, temperature differences show up as different colours ranging from hot (white) to cold (blue). This parked car's bonnet and wheels are still warm, indicating that the car has been driven not long before.

## Thermal imaging

All living things give off heat which can be detected by an electronic device called a thermal imager. This can produce a heat picture at night or in poor visibility and can detect the presence of heat through building walls. Thermal imagers are used on the ground or the air to detect missing animals, people and suspects or convicts on the run.

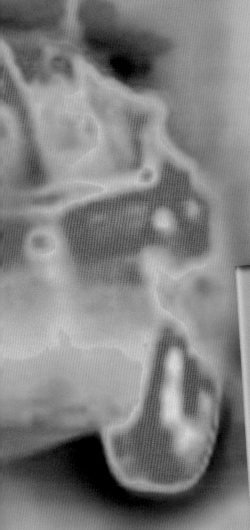

▲▶ A thermal imager is ideal for undercover work, or for searching for a suspect or fugitive without alerting them. Here, a law enforcement officer has spotted a suspect crouching near a wall.

## Driven

Law enforcement agents may feel the hood of a car to see if the engine is giving off heat, indicating that it was used recently. A thermal imager can sweep an area and determine which vehicle in a street of parked cars has the hottest exhaust or engine – indicating that the driver is nearby.

## Body heat

A healthy human body operates at a temperature of 37°C. After death, however, the body begins to lose heat until it reaches the temperature of the surrounding area. By measuring the temperature of the body when it is found, investigators can use this data to calculate the approximate time of death.

## Investigate

A cup of tea is found at a crime scene. It's still warm and the use of a thermometer and heat loss graph can determine when it was made. You will need a kettle, a cup, a thermometer for liquids, a stopwatch (or second hand on a watch) and a pencil and graph paper.

1 Place the thermometer in a recently made cup of tea and take a temperature reading.

2 Using the stopwatch, take a reading every 3 minutes and record the data (minutes and temperature.

3 Repeat the process until the temperature of the tea no longer changes. Then, using the data, plot a heat loss graph with Time running along the bottom, and Temperature running along the vertical.
Later, get someone to make a cup of tea without you knowing exactly when they did this (within 3 and 30 minutes). By taking the temperature and using your heat loss graph you can calculate approximately when the drink was made.

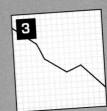

# Bullets and blood

Violent crimes often leave behind important clues, even when criminals have tried to remove all the evidence. When guns have been used, bullets, casings and gunshot residue can help detectives determine if a suspect fired the weapon, or was present at the scene. Some crimes also result in blood being spilled. Even when criminals have attempted to scrub it from their clothes, however, traces often remain. These can be identified by various techniques and connect a suspect with a crime.

## Going ballistic

Ballistics – the study of bullets and firearms – has a long history in forensic science, dating back to 1889. Today, information, including each gun's unique serial number, is collected in large computer database systems such as NIBIN (National Integrated Ballistic Information Network) in the USA. These help experts match bullets and cartridge casings to specific guns and owners.

▲ When a bullet shatters glass, it makes a distinctive pattern. This can help identify the precise location from which the gun was fired.

## Grooves and gunshots

When a gun is fired, microscopic scratches, caused by grooves on the barrel, are left on the bullet. These scratch marks, called striations, are unique to every firearm. If a gun is recovered, detectives can establish whether it was used to fire bullets found at the scene. Gunshot residue is also produced when a gun is fired. The residue can be swabbed from the skin or clothing to determine whether a suspect used the gun.

### A bloody business

Blood is analysed in a number of different ways. The blood is tested for its blood group (A, AB, B and O) which can help rule out a particular person. Blood can also be used in DNA testing (*see* pp 54-55). The pattern of blood stains and marks at a crime scene may be gruesome, but they can help investigators build up a detailed picture about a crime (*see* right).

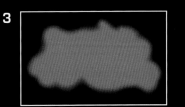
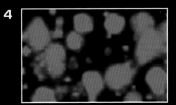

▲ Trails of blood can show how a crime may have developed (1). Spots with long tails indicate the victim was moving (2). A smeared bloodstain (3) may indicate the body has been dragged. Large spots (4) mean that the victim was moving slowly.

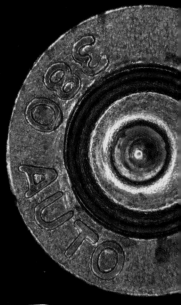

► Marks on a recovered bullet can be used to identify the weapon that fired it.

▲ A gun is fired during a ballistics test to determine whether it was used in a crime. Grooves, called rifling, inside the barrel of the gun leave unique marks on the bullet.

### Revealing the invisible

Special chemicals, such as fluorescin and luminol, can reveal the presence of blood even if it's invisible to the naked eye. Luminol glows when it comes into contact with blood. In a darkened room it can reveal minute traces of blood. Fluorescin is even more sensitive but needs a UV light source to make it glow.

## On the case

Two gunmen, Jason James and Daniel Whyte, shot and killed Giuseppina Martorana in Hertfordshire, UK, in 2000, when trying to steal her Rolex wristwatch. Firearm discharge residue, matching residue on the victim, was found on a duffle coat belonging to James. The two men were arrested and sentenced to life imprisonment.

# Signs left behind

Clues and evidence aren't found only at the primary crime scene but also where criminals live, work or hide. Many criminals attempt to conceal stolen items or incriminating evidence in ingenious ways, such as false bottoms in car boots and luggage.

In many countries, police have to obtain a legal document called a warrant to search a person's home. They do this when they have strong cause to believe that a search will reveal major evidence that could lead to a conviction.

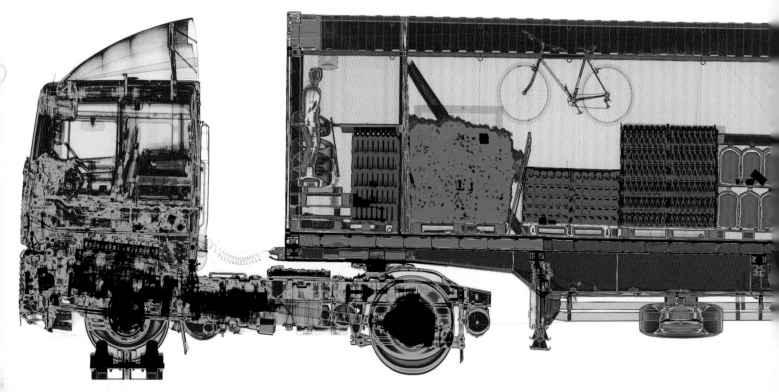

◀ Electrostatic detection apparatus (ESDA) uses static electricity and toner, which is sprinkled over the paper. This reveals impressions left by writing on the sheet above.

## Drawing a blank?

When a person writes on a sheet of paper, tiny marks made by the pen or pencil on the top sheet will show up on the sheet below. Even if the original sheet with writing has been destroyed, a device called ESDA (electrostatic detection apparatus) can make the writing visible.

## Secrets in the rubbish

Police officers at a crime scene or a suspect's lair carefully investigate gardens for freshly dug earth as well as garbage cans and wastebins for incriminating clues that haven't been destroyed. Sometimes, the evidence is immediately apparent such as bloodstained clothing or a weapon. Investigators are also on the look out for less obvious evidence – for example, shop receipts for items which might be connected to the crime.

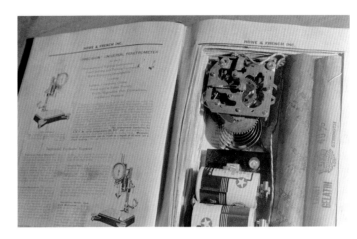

▲ Criminals have devised many clever ways to conceal evidence. This home-made bomb was discovered in a specially adapted book, by US detectives in 1950.

◄ X-ray scanning can quickly detect illegal goods, firearms or even people who are being smuggled across borders. Here an unknown person has been spotted (far left) in this truck.

## Sniffing out the evidence

Crimefighters use a range of technologies, including X-ray scans and metal detectors to locate hidden evidence. Dogs can be trained to sniff out not just the scent of a missing person or body but also particular types of chemicals as well as explosives and drugs.

## Investigate

You will need:
A pad of paper, a biro and a pencil.

1 Ask a friend to pick a name and phone number at random from a phonebook and, secretly, to write the details down on the pad with the biro.

2 After the top sheet has been removed, take a heavy lead pencil and gently shade over the next page of the pad until the writing emerges. Use a phonebook to see if you can fill in any missing details such as an address.

# Seeds of a clue

Examine carefully your clothes and shoes after a visit to the local park or a day out in the countryside. You will probably find material ranging from soil stuck to your shoes to burrs and seeds on your socks and trousers. During a criminal investigation, this kind of evidence found in cars, on clothes and on other objects, can give detectives valuable leads.

## Plant identification

Forensic botanists study plants and seeds from crime scenes. Sometimes, their work can change the course of an investigation. For example, leaves and seeds found on a victim's body might not match the plants that grow at the crime scene. As a result, investigators might conclude that the murder was committed elsewhere and the body moved.

▲ A forensic scientist takes a sample of soil from a suspect's shoe. The soil, which might contain seeds, could link the suspect to the crime scene.

◄ Seeds found on suspects and at crime scenes are collected and brought into the laboratory for identification.

## A tight hold

Pollen grains are very small and often sticky. They can attach themselves to paper, clothing, skin and even to the inside of your nose. Pollen found on a suspect can sometimes be matched with plants that grow in a specific location. Evidence such as this may help to place the suspect at the crime scene. Scientists who study pollen and other microscopic plant matter, such as spores, are called forensic palynologists.

◄ Hollyhock pollen is revealed under a scanning electron microscope. The pollen is covered in tiny spikes which help it stick to objects.

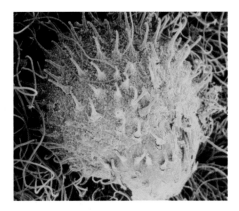

▲ A goosegrass burr contains a single seed inside an outer case with lots of tiny hooks or barbs. Here, it has become attached to wool from a suspect's clothes.

## Evidence of war crimes

From 1997 to 2001 a forensic team studied pollen samples from graves in Bosnia where there had been a bloody civil war. The team matched pollen from large mass graves to smaller graves. It proved important evidence in prosecuting Bosnian war criminals who tried to hide their acts of genocide by removing bodies from mass graves and reburying them in smaller or individual graves.

## On the case

Louise Almodovar was found strangled to death in New York's Central Park in 1942. Her husband, Anibal, claimed that he had not visited the park for over two years. The

police received a break when the eagle-eyed head of the city's Chemical And Toxicological Laboratory, Alexander O. Gettler, examined crime scene photos. He spotted that the grass on which the victim lay was not only very rare (it grew nowhere else in New York) but also that it was a late bloomer and only produced its seeds in October and November – the time of the murder. Anibal Almodovar's trousers and pockets contained many examples of these seeds. Faced with the evidence, he broke down and confessed to the murder.

# Hair, fibres and dust

Every single day, you shed up to 150 hairs! A hair discovered at the scene of a crime can help narrow down the search for suspects. Forensic analysis can show if the hair has been bleached or coloured. It can give clues to a person's gender and ethnic background. Fibres from clothing, and even dust, can also prove important evidence.

## Animals clues

Animal hairs can sometimes prove as useful as human hairs in solving a case. Forensic scientists can accurately identify the species of animal, and even its breed. This can make all the difference when the victim is a pet owner. Hairs from the pet may have become transferred to the suspect.

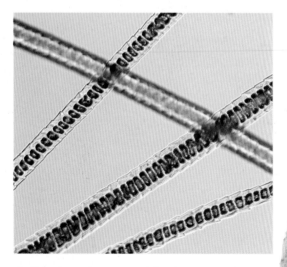

▲ Four hairs from a cat (*above*) and a single human hair (*right*) are viewed under high magnification microscopes. Human hairs can be tested to identify the presence of drugs.

### Matching fibres

There are thousands of different types of fibres – natural and artificial. A single strand can be enough to connect a suspect with a victim. Fibres helped convict British murderer Leonard Mills for the murder of Mabel Tattershaw in 1951. Hair discovered on the body of his victim matched his head and a blue thread under the victim's fingernail matched the fibres of Mills' suit.

### Dusty evidence

For detectives, even dust can reveal useful information. Brick dust found on a murder victim's clothes or at a crime scene, for example, might suggest that the victim had recently visited a building site. Dust can be lifted from surfaces with tape or a special vacuum device.

▲ This magnified image shows the fibres of a cotton t-shirt. Forensic scientists can identify the dye used to colour fibres by separating out the dye's components with chromatography.

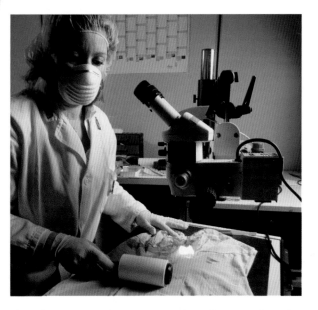

▲ A forensic scientist uses a sticky roller to pick up hair and fibres from a victim's dress. She wears protective clothing and gloves to avoid contaminating any evidence.

## On the case

In 1960 the body of a young boy, Graeme Thorne, was discovered, wrapped in a rug, 16km from his home in Sydney, Australia. The rug was covered in seeds from a rare type of cypress tree, unusual pink cement grains and hairs. These were later shown to come from a Pekinese dog. Detectives began searching for houses with the rare tree and unusual pink mortar. At the house of Stephen Bradley, a former Pekinese owner, they found a photograph of the rug and the dog. Bradley was caught on the run and later convicted of Thorne's murder.

# Marks, tears and breaks

When a crime takes place, damage often results. During a break-in, for example, a window might be smashed or a door forced off its hinges. Officers closely examine such details to build up a clearer picture of the crime. They might also reassemble damaged objects in a process called physical matching.

◀ A forced entry leaves behind crucial evidence such as broken glass. Detectives can quickly establish if the glass was smashed from the inside or the outside.

## Torn paper

Physical matching was used as early as 1784, in the UK, when John Toms was convicted of shooting and killing Edward Culshaw. A piece of torn newspaper was discovered inside the barrel of the murder weapon. The paper, which was used to hold gunpowder, matched perfectly the torn newspaper found in Toms's pocket.

▶ Physical matching can be used to put two or more pieces of a broken or torn item together. The item could be a piece of clothing, a letter, a smashed vase or, here, a torn cheque.

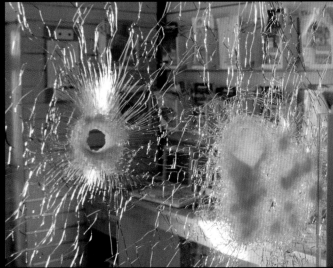

▲ An armed raid has left this distinctive pattern of bullet holes and shattered glass. Detectives take samples of the glass in case it matches fragments found on a suspect's clothes or in a getaway vehicle that has been recovered.

◄ A forensic scientist uses a microscope to compare paint chips from a car involved in an accident with known samples of paint. Finding a match can make identifying the car easier.

## Leaving your mark

After a burglary or break-in, officers check all the openings to a building for signs of forced entry. A drilled-out lock, a smashed window pane or marks around a window frame, where a tool such as a screwdriver or crowbar has been used, are classic signs. When marks are left behind, further examination can sometimes reveal the tool or object that made the mark.

## Paint

If paint samples are left at a crime scene by a car that has hit an object or a person, investigators might be able to trace the make and model of the vehicle involved. The Paint Database Query, used by police forces across the world, has information on over 50,000 layers of paints and 13,000 vehicles.

## On the case

A burglar and violent attacker became known as 'The Fox' for his ability to outwit police in the south of England in the mid-1980s. Visiting the scene of yet another brutal assault, in the village of Brampton, police discovered paint flakes, left by a car as it scraped past a tree. The paint was analysed and found to be the colour 'harvest gold', used only on one type of car – Austin Allegros made between 1973 and 1975. This helped narrow the search. When police visited Malcolm Fairley's house in North London they found him outside washing his car, a 'harvest gold' Allegro, complete with paint damage matching the paint found at the scene. Fairley confessed and was given life imprisonment.

# Making an impression

Impressions or prints made by feet, shoes, animal paws and tyre treads can yield vital data for forensic scientists. They can reveal the number of people at a crime scene or hideout, the type of vehicles used or even help uncover the identity of a victim or criminal. Shoeprints and footprints can be as distinctive as fingerprints. They are made when a person walks across snow, sand or soil, or steps in blood, paint or dust, leaving a clear impression.

◀▲ Impressions made by a shoe in soft ground are measured, photographed and cast. The exact make and type of shoe can be determined by checking shoe patterns stored on a database.

## Recording impressions

Forensic scientists take casts of shoe prints, footprints, tyre tracks and other impressions made in soft ground. These can be examined back at the laboratory. On dusty surfaces, foot and shoeprint impressions can be collected with a device called an electrostatic dust lifter.

## Comparing prints

Detectives can compare scans of shoeprints found at a crime scene with information and patterns supplied by shoe manufacturers and stored on databases. Some systems can analyse worn shoes for unique patterns of wear or marks made in the sole.

◀ Under UV light, a latent shoeprint is made visible. It is photographed and measured so it can be compared to a suspect's shoes.

▶ TreadMate is an advanced database which contains details of over 5,000 vehicle tyres.

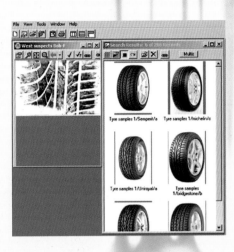

## The way you walk

A trail of footprints or shoeprints found at a crime scene can be studied to throw light on physical characteristics such as a suspect's stride length, evidence of a limp, and if toes point inwards. Details about the way a person walks can help detectives identify, or rule out, a suspect.

## Tyre tracks

Like shoes, tyres often leave a distinctive print or track. If detectives can match tread patterns with a suspect's vehicle they can establish if it was present at the scene. Databases allow tread patterns to be compared with thousands of tyre types, some designed for a specific car or motorbike.

◀ Investigators at a road accident can measure skidmarks to help calculate the speed of the vehicle when it lost control.

# Mystery substances

A briefcase is opened by detectives at a crime scene. A bottle containing an unidentified powder is found inside. Is it poison, an explosive, a powerful sleeping agent or an illegal drug? Investigators will soon have an answer as forensic science has developed powerful tools and tests to identify substances.

▲ A police officer checks readings from a chemical agent detector. This can identify dangerous gases.

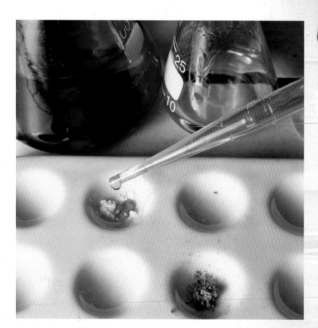

▲ Illegal drugs are tested in a lab. The white drug turns blue, indicating that it is cocaine. The brown drug is hashish, obtained from the cannabis plant.

## Drug testing

A range of different tests are used, some at the crime scene, to determine if a substance is a drug, or narcotic. For example a liquid mixture of formaldehyde and sulphuric acid turns purple in the presence of heroin or morphine. Back at the lab, scientists can use techniques such as gas chromatography to reveal the narcotic's precise make-up and discover clues about its origin.

▲ A law-enforcer in Washington, US, uses a mobile robot, which can be controlled from a safe distance. The robot can remove suspicious packages that may contain explosives or poisonous chemicals.

## Gas chromatography

Gas chromatography can pinpoint the identity of a substance by breaking it down into its chemical ingredients. It can be used to test for drugs, poisons and explosives. In 1988, the technique found the presence of chemicals used in Semtex, a powerful explosive, following the mid-air explosion of Pan Am flight 103. The investigation turned from accident to murder.

## Poisons

Poisoning has a long and notorious history. In Ancient Rome, poisoning was rife and accounted for the deaths of many Roman emperors. Today, poison cases are relatively rare. However, most known poisons leave a recognizable trace that can be detected during an autopsy.

▶ Crystals of arsenic disulphide are revealed under a microscope. This substance is a powerful poison and can also be used in explosives.

# Investigate

This simple test determines if a substance is an acid or base (alkali).

You will need a metal grater, half a head of red cabbage, a large saucepan, strainers and glass jar, an empty ice cube tray, an eye dropper or teaspoon.

**1** Grate the cabbage into the saucepan, add water and boil for 20–30 minutes until the liquid becomes dark purple. Strain and let the juice cool.

**2** Place some lemon juice, baking soda, vinegar and distilled water into the different compartments of the ice cube tray.

**3** Use the eye dropper or teaspoon to place six drops of cabbage juice into each compartment. Note the change in colour of the substances in each compartment and compare the results with the chart below.

| Baking soda | light green | slightly base |
|---|---|---|
| Lemon juice | red | acid |
| Vinegar | pink | slightly acid |
| Distilled water | purple | neutral |

# Fakes and counterfeits

Criminals produce fakes of all kinds of objects, from stamps to antique furniture. This criminal activity might consist of one person acting alone to sell fake artefacts to tourists. At the other end of the scale, there are sophisticated criminal networks that produce and traffic counterfeit currency in vast amounts.

▼ A Euro banknote is placed under ultraviolet light to reveal some of its security features. These include special fluorescent ink that glows bright blue or red under the light.

## Piracy and fakes

Creating illegal copies of items such as DVDs, CDs and computer software is big criminal business. Together with fake branded goods, such as watches and designer clothing, they are produced in huge quantities. In the UK, for example, 3 million pirated DVDs were seized in 2004. The sale of these illegal goods helps fund other criminal activities and damages legitimate businesses. In the US, the film industry loses around $3 billion a year from pirated DVDs.

▲ A technician studies US dollar banknotes to see whether they are genuine or fake. The US dollar is one of the most counterfeited of currencies because it is used across the world.

## Security features

To beat the counterfeiters, banknotes come with many security features. In the US, notes are printed on special paper that contains tiny coloured fibres. Even so, one forger managed to get round this by bleaching $1 bills and forging $100 notes on the blank paper. Other banknotes, such as the Euro, used in many European countries, have holograms which change in appearance when viewed from different angles. These are very hard to copy accurately.

## Counterfeit currency

Creating fake banknotes and coins is called counterfeiting. It has a long criminal history. During the American Civil War (1861–65), for example, over one-third of all the currency in circulation was counterfeit. Catching counterfeiters begins with detecting forged notes and then tracing their path back. Forensic scientists analyze the paper, ink and printing methods used in counterfeiting as well as tracing the serial numbers that identifies every individual banknote.

▲ Fake designer sunglasses are crushed by a bulldozer in Bangkok, Thailand. South East Asia is a major source of fake goods, ranging from pirated DVDs to clothing.

## On the case

Archaeological finds can also be faked. Piltdown Man, discovered in 1912, consisted of skull fragments and a jawbone of a creature claimed to be the missing link between apes and humans. It caused a sensation at the time. However, 41 years later, staff at the British Museum and at other institutions revealed it was a fake. Close examination showed that Piltdown Man had a human skull which had an orangutan jaw fitted with chimpanzee teeth. To this day, its creator remains unknown.

# Forgery or genuine?

A forgery is the illegal act of creating a false document. These documents range from fake passports and ID cards to entire books and diaries. If there are genuine documents connected to a crime, such as ransom notes, these are analysed for clues that might lead investigators to the culprit.

◀ Many forgers add words or numbers to an existing document. Here a zero has been added to this cheque. This is a very common type of forgery.

## Ink and paper analysis

Careful study of the ink and paper can show if a document has been tampered with, as well as if it is real or fake. Chemical analysis can reveal the exact type of paper used and even its age. Investigators can also compare the ink found in the document with a database of known inks to make a match. Documents are also examined for fingerprints and other trace evidence.

## Handwriting

Handwriting experts employ various techniques to distinguish between a genuine document and a forgery. They study characteristics such as the shape, size and the angle of letters and words. In top letter analysis, the highest point of each letter is joined. The resulting 'graph' is compared for similarities with one made from a document that is known to be original.

▼ Different inks absorb and reflect light in different ways. Video spectral comparison uses special light sources to establish whether the ink used throughout a document is the same.

▶ An investigator examines passports and other identity documents. Genuine documents have security features which are very hard to forge.

## All in the content

For some documents, such as ransom demands or threatening letters, experts called linguistic analysts can examine the content. They look for patterns of words, certain phrases and other clues about the writer's origin. Repeated spelling or punctuation mistakes may also help lead investigators to a particular suspect.

# On the case

The German magazine *Stern* created a sensation in 1983 when it ran extracts allegedly from Adolf Hitler's secret diaries. The magazine had paid a German dealer, Konrad Kujau, £2.1 million for the diaries. Forensics experts, however, found that the diary's paper contained a whitening chemical only introduced in 1954, nine years after Hitler's death. Analysis also showed that the ink wasn't available when Hitler was alive. The trail led back to Kujau who was convicted of forging the diaries and sentenced to four and a half years in prison.

# Art forgery

An art collector can pay a fortune for a painting but it won't necessarily be the genuine article! Art experts estimate that ten percent of pictures in circulation are forgeries. But can the fakes fool the experts?

▼ Master forger Tom Keating left deliberate clues in his forgeries, such as writing on the canvas which could be seen under X-rays.

## Homework

To produce convincing forgeries, art forgers study the originals in great detail. They mimic the technique of the artist they are copying in every way, including the exact style of brush stroke.

▼ Microscopes can indicate tiny hairline cracks on the surface of old paintings. Experts can tell the difference between real and fake cracks.

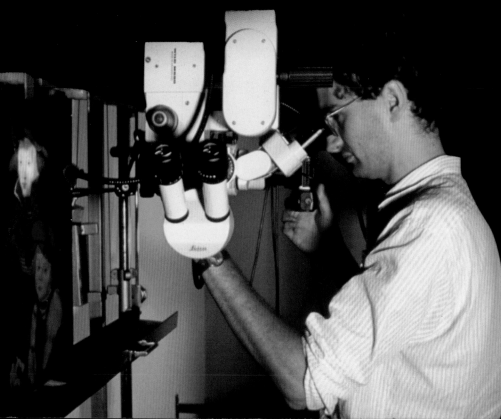

## Under the surface

Forensic scientists analyse the fingerprints and palm prints that are often left in a painting. Paintings can also be X-rayed or scanned to look for clues. Some artists build up a painting from many layers. Others only use one layer. By comparing a suspect painting to a genuine original by the same artist, it is often possible to spot a forged painting.

▲ An infrared scan highlights a small section of the painting. This can reveal hidden details that are invisible to the naked eye.

▲ This painting is a copy of an original. Under ultraviolet light an area (indicated by the red circle) appears darker than the rest of the painting, confirming that it has been retouched or painted over.

## You've been framed

Many forgeries can be identified by art experts from the materials used. Forgeries of paintings from the 17th century, for example, have been made using paints only invented in the 20th century. Carbon dating can unmask a modern copy of an old artwork by revealing the age of a frame or canvas. Some forgers get round this by using frames and canvases from the correct period.

## On the case

Henricus Antonius van Meegeren, a Dutch painter, began to produce extremely accurate forgeries of Vermeer paintings in the 1930s that convinced a number of art experts and made him rich. After World War II, van Meegeren was undone. Accused of working with the German Nazis by selling them genuine paintings, he proved that the paintings were fakes by producing a new painting in front of astonished police officers. Van Meegeren was sentenced to one year in jail but died before he went to prison.

# Fire!

Firefighters have put out a fierce house fire. Forensic investigators have arrived at the scene and begun to sift through the smouldering debris. They are looking for clues that might indicate the cause of the fire. Criminals can use fires to try to cover up their crimes by making them look like an accident or to destroy important evidence. When a fire is started deliberately, it is called arson.

▶ Dogs have an extremely sensitive sense of smell. Some have been trained to sniff out accelerants, such as petrol, at fire scenes.

▲ Arson can have devastating results. This fire in a New York club, in 1990, killed 87 people. It was started by Julio Gonzalez who had been thrown out of the club earlier in the evening.

## Take a seat

The place where a fire started is called the seat. It is often where the blaze is fiercest. An accidental fire, caused by a cigarette or a faulty electrical appliance, is likely to have just one seat. Arsonists, however, often try to start several fires in different places. Investigators can plot the path of a fire by examining burn patterns and the extent of the damage in different parts of the building.

## Firestarters

Arson investigators are on the look out for accelerants – substances that help speed up a fire or increase the size and strength of a blaze. Common accelerants are wood kindling, paint thinners and petrol. Incendiary devices such as matches, explosives or a lighter can also indicate that the fire is a clear case of arson.

► Computers can accurately reconstruct how a fire develops. This can help investigators establish its cause.

► Two minutes after a fire began in the basement (see image), it has spread through a number of parts of the house.

## Cover-up

Covering up a crime by making it look an accident or burning evidence such as a victim's clothes or important documents, are just two reasons why a fire may be started. Investigators at a suspected arson scene must consider all the possibilities.

## Burning motives

Some fires are started out of anger or revenge. Others by owners of struggling businesses in order to claim money on insurance. Fire investigators usually run background checks on people connected with the building in order to uncover any possible motives.

▼ Fires often result in widespread destruction. Over a third of all fires are caused by arson.

# Technology at work

Forensic science drives many advances in technology. Crime-fighters today have at their disposal a huge range of ingenious and powerful techniques. Some are used in everyday crime investigations. Others have their place in forensic laboratories.

▲ A forensic scientist uses a comparison microscope and a computer database called Bulletproof to match the markings on a fired bullet with one held in the records.

## Bullet proof

In order to combat the rise of gun crime in many countries there have been a number of major technological developments. For example, Kevlar, a material used in protective body armour which prevents a bullet from reaching the skin, has saved many lives. In the laboratory, bullets can be analysed and quickly matched with a particular firearm.

## Keeping watch

Close observation of suspects, or surveillance, plays a key role in crime-fighting. Some law-enforcement agencies can apply for the right to put suspects under surveillance using electronic taps of their telephone and monitoring their emails. In some cases, they bug a suspect's home or workplace with tiny, hidden cameras and microphones.

▼ A laser beam (red) can map with great accuracy the path of a bullet, or its trajectory. This technique can pinpoint the exact location from where a gun was fired.

◀ This close-up of a scanning electron microscope (SEM) shows where a sample is placed and bombarded with electrons. SEMs can magnify objects up to 10,000 times.

## Seeing the invisible

Forensic scientists use powerful instruments to find and investigate the smallest traces of tell-tale evidence. Scanning electron microscopes (SEMs) are powerful microscopes that send out a beam of electrons. SEMs allow users to study the tiniest details on the surface of a substance such as a pollen grain or gunshot residue.

▲ This SEM shows the shell of a dermestid beetle that was found in the hair of a dead body. This beetle feeds on bodies about two months after death. The study of these insects can give valuable clues about the time of death.

# Power to the computer

Today, there are hundreds of millions of personal computers (PCs) in use across the world, many linked by computer networks or the internet. This has resulted in wave after wave of computer-based crime. But computers have also enabled crime-fighters to counter criminals in new and innovative ways.

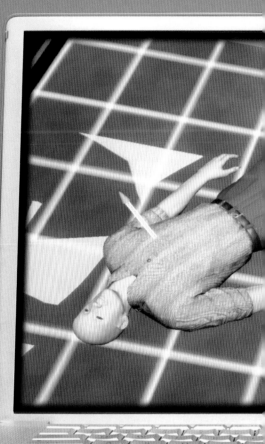

▶ Using powerful computer software, a crime scene is reconstructed. The yellow arrow shows the trajectory of the bullet that killed the victim. The position of broken glass can also be seen. Analysts can view the scene from all angles to help determine where the killer was standing.

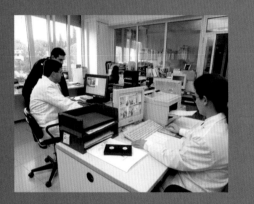

▲ Investigators examine CCTV footage of a crime stored on a crime analysis database. This gives them access to data and images about current and past crimes so that they can detect any similarities.

## Screen time

Computers have revolutionized almost every aspect of forensic science. They can produce, for example, very realistic facial reconstructions and identikit images of suspects and missing persons. They are also used to re-create crime scenes or to generate an animated sequence of a car crash that can give investigators valuable insights.

## Information exchange

Sharing information is crucial in order to get ahead of criminals. Law-enforcement agencies across the world depend on computer networks to exchange crime-fighting data, from fingerprint details to criminal records of suspects.

▶ A detective removes a computer from a crime scene. It has been wrapped to preserve fingerprints. Back at the laboratory, investigators will retrieve data from the machine's hard drive.

## Hacking, theft and viruses

Computers hold vast amounts of data about people and organizations. Criminals can take advantage of this by hacking, or breaking into, computer systems. Their aim is to steal funds or information. Hackers can also sabotage computers by releasing computer viruses.

▲ A hacker attempts to gain access and control of other people's computers over the internet. It has been estimated that cybercrime is worth more than the international illegal drugs trade.

## Electronic evidence

Criminals sometimes store incriminating information on computers, personal digital assistants (PDAs) or mobile phones. Computer forensics is the collection and analysis of this electronic evidence. Experts can recover data from hard disks or memory cards, even if they have been wiped clean. They also track down individuals who have hacked into other people's computers.

## On the case

Many crimes involve the use of computers for blackmail, theft or fraud. In 2004, for example, Phillip Shortman, a British teenager, defrauded users of the eBay auction website. He recieved money for goods he did not own and that were never sent to the winning bidders. Shortman, who collected over £45,000 from unsuspecting bidders, was sentenced in 2005 to one year's detention.

# DNA profiling

DNA, or deoxyribonucleic acid, is a chemical found in most cells of the human body. Everybody's DNA is different, apart from identical twins. It has become an essential tool for crime-fighters trying to identify victims and criminals.

▼ Unravelled, a strand of DNA looks like a spiralling ladder. If DNA from a suspect matches a sample found at a crime scene, it is very likely the individual was present.

▼ When DNA has been cut up and processed it produces a unique banding pattern that can be seen in X-ray photographs, or autoradiographs.

## DNA samples

DNA can be extracted from any body fluid, including blood, sweat or saliva. It is present in every part of the body – a tiny piece of skin or a single hair root, discovered at a crime scene, is enough to provide a sample. Once the DNA has been extracted and analysed it can be compared to any other sample to determine if it has come from the same person.

## Processing DNA

DNA profiling does not use the whole of a person's DNA. Scientists focus on shorter repeating patterns found in DNA that are known to vary greatly among individuals. DNA is taken from the nucleus of a cell. It is then cut into smaller sections, sorted, processed and photographed using X-ray film. The resulting record is stored on a database.

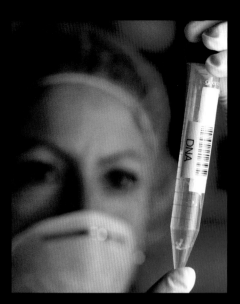

▶ A forensic scientist holds up a vial containing DNA discovered at a crime scene. The DNA is isolated from other material found in the cell by applying chemicals or a salt solution.

## Room for doubt

If a match is made there is a very strong probability that the samples came from the same person. However, DNA profiling, while a powerful tool, is not perfect. Critics argue that samples are small and that there is a risk of mistakes being made. Ideally, there should be other strong evidence to support DNA findings.

## On the case

Two girls from Leicestershire, UK, were murdered, one in 1983 and another in 1986. The murders were the first in which DNA evidence was vital in solving the case. Police took DNA samples from some 4,500 men in the local area to compare with samples found at the murder scenes. One local man, Colin Pitchfork, persuaded a friend to give a sample in his place. Police discovered this fact. When a sample was taken from Pitchfork, it matched the samples found at the murder scene. In 1988 Pitchfork, who pleaded guilty to both murders, was sentenced to life imprisonment.

# DNA in action

DNA profiling is used for older cases as well as current criminal investigations. DNA techniques, which might not have been available at the time, can shed dramatic new light on the evidence. DNA techniques are also applied to creatures other than humans in the fight against poaching and smuggling.

## Case closed?

DNA profiling has seen many old or unsolved cases successfully concluded. In 2002, in the UK, Operation Magnum used DNA profiling to link three murders committed in 1973 to one man. However, as some cases are finally closed, others are re-opened. DNA profiling can provide new evidence which may prove that the person convicted of a crime was, in fact, innocent. In the US, as a result of DNA testing, over 140 people have be cleared of crimes for which they had been convicted.

▼ Investigators check DNA autoradiographs. They are looking for a match between two samples in order to prove a connection.

## Animal detectives

One of the foremost centres for DNA work on wildlife is the National Fish and Wildlife Forensics Laboratory in Oregon, US. The first lab in the world dedicated to solving wildlife crimes, it handles around 900 cases every year. Typical cases involve illegal hunting, animal smuggling and the killing of protected species for their fur, horn or other body parts.

## Eco forensics

In crimes involving animals or the environment, investigators use a wide array of forensic techniques. Bullet matching, tyre track analysis and animal blood analysis may lead investigators to the killer of protected species. Environmental investigators may use satellite imagery, chemical testing and witness statements to track down, for example, illegal waste dumping.

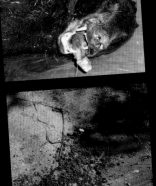

▶ A bear, killed by poachers, is brought back to the lab to determine how it died.

▶ DNA analysis of blood found by a roadside can establish the species of animal. A match may be made with blood found on a suspect's clothes.

## On the case

In December 2005, Australia's most notorious murder case of recent years came to an end. Bradley Murdoch was found guilty of the 2001 murder of British backpacker, Peter Falconio who had been travelling with his girlfriend in a camper van. At the heart of the prosecution's case was DNA evidence. The court heard that a sample of DNA found on homemade handcuffs used in the attack was 100 million times more likely to have come from Murdoch than from anyone else.

# Where to next?

## Books

*Hidden Evidence* by David Owen (Quintet Publishing, 2001)

*Forensics: True Crime Scene Investigations* by Dr Zakaria Erzinçlioglu (Carlton Publishing, 2004)

*The Forensics Handbook* by Pete Moore (Eye Books, 2004)

*Crime Scene* by Richard Platt (Dorling Kindersley, 2003)

*Forensics For Dummies* by D.P. Lyle (Wiley Publishing, 2004)

*Fingerprints and Talking Bones* by Charlotte Foltz Jones (Bantam Doubleday Dell, 1997)

*Detective Science* by Jim Wiese (John Wiley & Sons, 1996)

*Forensic Science* by Andrea Campbell (Chelsea House Publishers, 2000)

*The Forensic Casebook* by N.E. Genge (Ballantine, 2004)

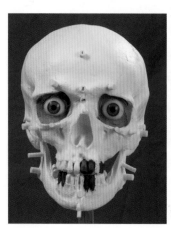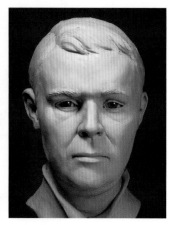

## Websites

www.fbi.gov/fbikids.htm
The Federal Bureau of Investigation (FBI) website includes some fascinating pages on how the agency works and run-throughs of typical cases. The webpages are split into sections for children and young adults.

www.crimelibrary.com/criminal_mind/forensics/art/1.html
The crimelibrary website takes a detailed look at forensic artists and photographers.

www.channel4.com/science/microsites/S/science/society/forensic_marks.html
A microsite from Channel 4 that has features on marks and other evidence found at a crime scene.

www.bbc.co.uk/crime/caseclosed/forensics.shtml
These webpages from the BBC focus on the use of DNA fingerprinting.

www.discoverychannel.co.uk/crime/_home/index.shtml
A great website from the Discovery Channel, which explains the roles of forensic scientists and other investigators, as well as highlighting the different techniques that they use.

http://www.planet-science.com/whodunit/go/TheCase/Default
A fun online investigation brought to you by Planet Science in which you get to examine clues and use crime-solving techniques.

www.odci.gov/cia/ciakids
This section of the Central Intelligence Agency's (CIA) website is aimed at young adults.

www.reachoutmichigan.org/funexperiments/
agesubject/lessons/prints.html
At this website, you can learn more about
examining and classifying fingerprints, with links
to other useful fingerprinting webpages.

www.pito.org.uk
This website, run by the Police Information
Technology Organisation, outlines the latest
developments in high-tech crime-fighting.

www.met.police.uk/links/index.htm
This wide-ranging collection of links to police
forces and other crime-fighting resources is
hosted by London's Metropolitan Police.

www.crimelibrary.com/criminal_mind/forensics/
ballistics/3.html
This crimelibrary feature examines the role of
ballistics in solving violent crimes.

www.abc.net.au/science/slab/forensic/default.htm
This website provides an excellent verview of the
techniques crime-fighters use to solve cases.

www.pbs.org/opb/historydetectives/case/
208_forgers.html
To learn more about fakes and forgeries, go to
this website produced by US broadcaster PBS.

# Glossary

**Accelerant**
A substance used to make a fire burn more fiercely.

**Arson**
The crime of deliberately setting fire to something with intent to injure or destroy.

**Autopsy**
Also known as a post-mortem, the examination of a body to find the cause of death.

**Ballistics**
The study of how bullets and other missiles travel through the air and materials, and their examination for distinctive characteristics after being fired.

**Chromatography**
The process of separating a chemical mixture, such as ink, into its individual substances.

**Computer virus**
A compute program or piece of computer code that can make copies of itself. Some computer viruses are harmful, copying data to other computers or erasing it.

**Counterfeit**
An imitation or copy of an object, document or banknote.

**Database**
Information stored on a computer so that it can be searched and easily accessed.

**Defendant**
The person in court accused by the prosecution of committing a crime.

**DNA**
Short for deoxyribonucleic acid, a chemical in the cells of living things that carries genetic information.

**DNA profiling**
The process of testing a sample, for example blood found at a crime scene, to identify DNA that matches another sample.

**Dusting**
The application of powder to a fingerprint in order to reveal and lift it.

**Evidence**
Something that is used to prove that a crime has been committed, or that a particular person has committed the crime.

**Forensic anthropologist**
A specialist in examining skeletons, bones and other unidentified human remains.

**Forensic palynologist**
A person who studies pollen and other plant materials.

**Forensic science**
The application of science in the course of a criminal investigation.

**Gas chromatography**
The technique for separating out a substance and identifying its different ingredients by analysing the gases released when it is burned.

**Gunshot residue**
The traces of powder left behind after a gun has been fired.

## Hacker
A person who deliberately accesses private information on someone else's computer without that person's consent.

## Identikit image
A likeness of a person's face created from descriptions given to the police.

## Latent fingerprint
A full or partial fingerprint made by deposits of oils or sweat. Latent fingerprints are often only visible when chemicals or special lighting are used.

## Polygraph
A machine that helps an investigator determine whether someone is lying, by measuring body responses when the subject is questioned.

## Post-mortem
*See* autopsy.

## Prosecution
The team of lawyers who try to prove that the defendant in court is guilty of committing the crime or crimes.

## Rifling
A spiral-shaped raised pattern inside the barrel of a gun.

## Rigor mortis
Tension or stiffness that sets into the muscles of the body shortly after death.

## Scanning electron microscope (SEM)
A machine that generates three-dimensional images of an object at a very high magnification.

## Striations
Scratch-like grooves on a bullet that are created by the bullet travelling through a gun barrel.

## Surveillance
Observation of a person, usually a suspect, during a criminal investigation.

## Suspect
A person who may have committed a crime.

## Thermal imaging
A way of capturing infrared 'heat' energy to build up a picture of an object or scene.

## Toxicology
The study of poisons and drugs, and their effects on humans and animals.

## Trace evidence
Evidence found in tiny quantities.

## Tread pattern
The arrangement of groves and raised areas of a vehicle tyre. The term is also used to describe the pattern on the sole of shoes.

## Voiceprint
A way of representing the sound of a person's speech in the form of a graph.

## Witness
A person who may have seen or heard something of importance to a crime investigation.

## X-ray
A type of energy wave that is used to penetrate objects and living things to reveal what lies under the surface.

# Index

# Acknowledgements

KEY
t = top; c = centre; b = bottom; r = right; l = left

*The publishers would like to thank the following for permission to use their photographs:*

1 Smiths Detection; 2–3 Thames Valley Police; 4–5 Getty Images; 6 bl Getty Images; 7 tl Thames Valley Police; 7 r Getty Images/Photodisc; 8–9 TEK Image/Science Photo Library (SPL); 8 bl Thames Valley Police; 12–13 SPL; 12 bl Getty Images; 12 tl Human Identification Technologies, Inc., Redlands, CA; 14–15 Getty Images/Photodisc; 14 bl Mauro Fermariello/SPL; 15 tr Steven van Aperen; 16–17 Getty Images; 17 br Du Cane Medical Imaging Ltd/SPL; 18–19 Steria/Martin Faleby; 18 bl Steria/Martin Faleby;19 tr Mauro Fermariello/SPL ; 20 b Thames Valley Police; 21 tr Sandia National Laboratories/SPL; 22–23 Dr Iain A Pretty, University of Manchester Dental School; 24 bl Philippe Faraut/PCF Studios, Inc.; 25 tr Astrid & Hanns-Frieder Michler; 25 br Silkeborg Museum, Denmark/Munoz-Yague/SPL; 26–27 Ted Kinsman/SPL; 27 tr FLIR Systems; 28–29 Stephen Dalton/SPL; 28 bl Michael Donne/SPL; 29 cr Forensic Technology WAI Inc.; 30–31 Smiths Detection; 30 bl Giles Document Laboratory; 31 tr Getty Images; 32–33 Eye of Science/SPL; 32 cr Volker Steger, Peter Arnold Inc./SPL; 32 bl Bell Museum of Natural History, University of Minnesota; 33 tr Dr Jeremy Burgess/SPL; 34–35 Susumu Nishinaga/SPL; 34 bl McCrone Associates, Westmont, Illinois, and the Editor of the McCrone Atlas of Microscopic Particles, and ModernMicroscopy.com; 35 bl Mauro Fermariello/SPL; 35 tr Eye of Science/SPL; 36 l Getty Images; 36–37 tc Volker Steger, Peter Arnold Inc./SPL; 37 tr Michael Donne/SPL; 38–39 Thames Valley Police; 38 cl Foster and Freeman; 39 tr Foster and Freeman 39 br TRL Ltd; 40–41 Getty Images; 40 cl Mauro Fermariello/SPL; 40 tr Smiths Detection; 41 tr Andrew Syred/SPL; 42 Mauro Fermariello/SPL; 43 tl Michel Viard, Peter Arnold Inc./SPL; 43 cr Getty Images; 43 br John Reader/SPL; 44–45 Giles Document Laboratory; 45 cr Mauro Fermariello/SPL; 45 br Getty Images; 46–47 c Volker Steger/SPL; 46 c John Dee/Rex Features; 46 bl Volker Steger/SPL; 47 Volker Steger/SPL 48–49 c Corbis UK Ltd; 48 cl AP Photo; 48–49 t Michael Donne/SPL; 50–51 Colin Cuthbert/SPL; 50 cl Mauro Fermariello/SPL; Michael Viard, Peter Arnold Inc./SPL; 50 br; 51 br Volker Steger/SPL; 52 cl Mauro Fermariello/SPL; 52–53 Mauro Fermariello/SPL; 53 b TEK Image/SPL; 53 tr Getty Images; 54–55 Alfred Pasieka/SPL; 54 bl TEK Image/SPL; 55 tr Mauro Fermariello/SPL; 55 br Neville Chadwick/SPL; 56–57 Peter Menzel/SPL; 57 r Trent University Wildlife Forensic Laboratory, Ontario; 57 br Getty Images; 58 bl Philippe Faraut/PCF Studios, Inc.; 59 br Thames Valley Police.

All other photographs taken by Peter Clayman.

Illustration on 24–25 by Sebastian Quigley

*The author would like to thank Ann McDermott and Edward Nkune.*

*The publishers would like to thank the following: Mehul Anjaria, Steve van Aperen, Richard E. Bisbing, Anita Cholewa, Martin Faleby, Philippe Faraut, Tonja Fritz-Johnson, Anthony Gagliardi, Dr A Giles, Iain Pretty, Paul Sacker, WA Products, Linsay Weis.*